Saint Sinatra
& Other Poems

Saint Sinatra
& Other Poems

Poems by Angela Alaimo O'Donnell

Word Press

Published by Word Press
P.O. Box 541106
Cincinnati, OH 45254-1106

ISBN: 9781936370351
LCCN: 2011927808

Poetry Editor: Kevin Walzer
Business Editor: Lori Jareo

Visit us on the web at www.word-press.com

Cover Design: Paul Schutz

Acknowledgments

Acknowledgement is made to the following publications in which some of these poems have appeared or are forthcoming:

America: "St. Martha," "St. Seamus," "St. Vincent"
Christian Century: "And the Angel Left Her," "What the
       Angel Said," "St. Lazarus," "The Vigil"
Christianity and Literature: "St. Melville"
Comstock Review: "Saint Sinatra"
Journal of the Motherhood Initiative: "Homegoing"
Mezzo Cammin: "Homage to St. Edna: A Sonnenizio,"
       "Dear Heart"
Runes: A Review of Poetry: "St. Hawk and St. Shrew"
St. Katherine Review: "Letters to My Heart"
Vineyards: "Black Robe's Box"
Windhover: "Big Sur Saints," "The Conversation,"
       "Christ's Colors," "Peter's Glimpse,"
       "St. Eve in Exile," "St. Hawthorne," "St. Ikaros,"
       "St. Thomas," "The Long Run,"
       "Waiting for Ecstasy"

"Poet's Heresy" appeared in the anthology, *Poem Home,* and has been reprinted with the permission of Paper Kite Press.

The following poems appeared in a previous collection by the author, *Moving House,* and appear with the permission of Word Press:
       "Saints' Lives," "St. Melville,"
       "St. Ahab," and "Waiting for Ecstasy"

I want to extend heartfelt thanks to those who offered invaluable advice and encouragement in connection with these poems and this project, especially Alan Berecka, Michael Dennis Browne, Scott Cairns, Kelly Cherry, Kate Daniels, Paul Mariani, and Jeanne Murray Walker.

I'd also like to offer special thanks to David Craig at Franciscan University for publishing the chapbook, *Waiting for Ecstasy* (Franciscan Press, 2009) in which a number of these poems appear.

I am grateful to my colleagues at Fordham University, especially Mark Massa, Maria Terzulli, and Christine Firer Hinze, for their generous support of my work at the Curran Center, in the classroom, and at my writing desk. In addition, I am grateful to my students, whose intelligence and love of learning are a constant source of inspiration, energy, and joy.

Finally, I'd like to express my deepest gratitude to my family: to my sisters, Charlene and Rose Ann, and my brothers, Greg and Lou, who have embraced my work with great affection and enthusiasm; to my sons, Charles, Patrick, and Will, who have demonstrated long patience with their mother's poetic preoccupations and literary obsessions; and to my husband, Brennan, whose enduring love & friendship, in addition to his fine ear & unerring critical eye, are among my life's best blessings.

For my mother,
Marion Salvi Alaimo,
who loved the saints

Table of Contents

"The only tragedy in life is not to be a saint."
Leon Bloy

*"Lord, how I want to be in that
number."* Anonymous

Saint Sinatra

*"Saints are the most excellent of voices,
the most brilliant of stars." Avery Cardinal Dulles*

Croon to me, Baby,
blue-eyes smiling,

*So Easy to Love
Night and Day,*

skinny legs draped
in gabardine as you sway

sweet and easy, singing.
The mike your attribute,

lucky close to those lips,
In other words, baby, kiss me.

I've Got a Crush on You, Sweetie Pie,
You, Sicilian Saint of Song,

the one girls pray to when we lie
awake, pictures of boys in our heads,

each of them holy-card pretty as you
only *In the Blue of Evening.*

You and the Night and the Music
much more than we can stand,

we fall to our knobby knees,
genuflect to your smooth

slide down the scale of desire,
a true tune we know and can't carry.

O Hoboken Hero of Eros,
Star-eyed *Stranger in the Night,*

Pray for us, Sinner. Sing us alive.
Take these Valentine hearts from our hands.

I. Sisters

St. Eve in Exile

Here amid a field of light
You say my name.

And I am not she,
the girl You called Your own.

My mouth a cavern.
My chest an empty cave.

I am dry and dusty.
I am not wet or well.

Not the riverbed of love
You shaped me to be,

wide as a delta,
deep as any mine-

ful of diamonds,
not this common coal,

my birthstone, my rock
of heavy longing.

I am black with it
where You would have me white.

Ever a disappointment,
I grew breasts

where you shaped me straight and smooth,
spoke when you asked for a song,

agreed where you hoped
I would exceed,

climb out of the hole
You dug for me,

place where You planted
me in the dark

among creatures
who never knew my name.

You cut me in two.
I take half the blame.

What the Angel Said

for Fra Angelico on seeing his Annunciation,
Chiesa San Marco, Florence

He spoke to you in blue, in the long call
of light from the top of a Tuscan hill.
Your hand answered, the quick sketch of a girl
taking shape before you knew she was you,
head uplifted, her angelful eyes
sure of what they see: being bodied true
as the stilled wings, the beatified sky.
What words might have passed have passed as air
sighed by the soul in the act of rapture.
Now there is only ocher and thin-skinned cream,
struck gold against the garden's sudden green,
forever as present as it once seemed,
her hands crossed soft against her hidden fear
and angel's breath still warm within your ear.

St. Martha

"She had a sister called Mary, who was seated at the Lord's feet, listening to His word." Luke 10:37

A silly child she ever always was—
our mother said so a thousand times—
her quick eye caught by the flight or buzz
of some pretty creature's mastering wings.
Lazarus tried to keep her out of sight,
to spare his clever sister women's tasks.
I hauled the water, rose before first light,
set bread upon the board before they asked.
The day You came to us our prayers were granted.
My hands obeyed the rhythms of my labor
while Mary sat beside You like a man,
embraced within the circle of Your favor.
       I stood apart, Your beauty kept from me,
       and only when You left us did I see.

St. Kate
Siena, 1347-80

All the way to heaven is heaven,
laughed the golden girl,
24th child of 25.

She celled her self,
a rare fruit tree
blossoming behind rock walls.

Outside, the plague raged,
bodies piled high
to the tune of terrified cries.

So she came out
wearing Christ's foreskin
on her neat ring finger.

She kissed blackened
toes and buboes
and dared death.

She buried children merrily:
Two more I no longer
need to worry about!

She learned to be love
without love—
a perfect and perilous thing.

All she wanted was You.
What she got was
Every One.

She ate nothing
but souls
for 9 years.

She told the Pope
to come home
and be a man.

You laughed
in Your heaven.
You waited for her.

Out of Avila

"This is how I treat my friends,"
said a voice within me.
"Yes, my Lord," I replied, "and that is why
you have so few of them."—St. Theresa

Sharp-tongued sister,
quick with a quip,
the ready rejoinder,
the argument with God,

what made you equal
to the task,
mistress of wit
men lacked nerve enough to master?

They feared you, serious
Serious Sister, called
& hauled before High Priests
who wanted nothing

more than your secret
source of your power,
what you knew and who
you thought you were.

You kept your own
counsel, go-to girl,
mother-of-us-all,
free to speak when you would

for those who couldn't.
You laughed and prayed,
levitated and landed,
gave as good as you got.

Dis-calced, dis-reputable,
dis-missable, dis-trusted,
God knows, you were a talker.
So She named you *Doctor.*

Deutschland Saints

December 7ᵗʰ, 1875
After Gerard Manley Hopkins

The ship that lost them foundered on the hill
beneath the waves beyond the coast of Kent.
Her steel keel stopped by shards of shell,
her masts battered by the winds of Hell,
she shuddered as the last lights went
down in a western sea without mercy.
The five nuns cried, "Christ, quickly, come!"
beseeched an empty sky for the saving sun,
but died, at last, of cold and broken hearts.
They made their final peace with the sea
governed by the hidden star of Mary,
as she embraced them in the chilly air,
a mother well-practiced in her art
of saving saints and fools from their despair.

Heresy #1: Saints' Lives

Rape. A handful of pills. And it's over.
A brief life of skirts and curls,
slumber parties, sacramental signs.

Water, Chrism, the Body and the Slap.
Consummatum est, He said upon His cross.
But not like this, Lord, this girl's answer.

St. Maria Goretti denied him entry,
bled out upon the scullery floor.
Father, forgive him rung the copper pots.

St. Joan stood stoic, bound to fire and flame
reveling in the heat: *My God, my God,*
You will not forsake me. She was that sure.

St. Agatha's breasts, sliced and served.
St. Lucy's mild eyes upon the dish.
And St. Cecilia succumbed, they say, singing.

These girls all aglow with one desire
painted bright in hues of red and blue,
their fixed lips mouthing softly,
yes, yes, yes, O yes.

II. Brothers

Peter's Glimpse

And He was transfigured before them,
and his face shone like the sun.
       —St. Matthew 17:2

My understanding young, Lord, my hopes high.
The bright light misshapes you before our eyes,
and standing amazed seems all that we can do
as we watch and wait to recover and reclaim you.
No longer strangers, we are your second selves
seeing our souls flash forth in your light
caught up in the magnitude of our delight
falling in love with the love light tells.

Now how shall we see where to set our feet
as we make our way down the mountain's dark side,
our eyes still dazzled, our knowledge incomplete,
neither past nor present a trustworthy guide?
How will you light the road we do not know
once you have gone the way we have to go?

St. Francis and His Kin

Francis claimed Umbria, her earth and sky.
Instead of bread, he tasted daily blue.
He'd bless the cypress, greet the olive branch,
kiss the wind that stirred his naked thigh.

Francis stalked the hills steep with love.
He traced God's name on Assisi's wall,
begged Brother Fire to cauterize his eyes,
thumbed ash on the head of a morning dove.

Francis went blind and sang to Brother Sun
a hymn to light his heart could darkly see.
Noon breathed hot upon his outstretched hands,
bathed the tired body he used to be.

Brother Ass remained, faithful as the birds,
while Francis preached a gospel without words.

St. Thomas

"All that I have written seems to me like so much straw." St. Thomas
Aquinas, December 6, 1273

Mid-day mass in the old stone church,
the host hoisted high in my hands,
when winter light pierces my heart.

Conflagration an end
devoutly to be wished.
I watch as my decades of pages

catch fire in the late day light,
warming the chill
of this cold chapel.

I watch the black letters,
licked by the flames,
consumed in a glory of orange,

the blue light leap from each live leaf,
like straw strewn on the stable floor
touched by the match of Christ.

How could they not
dance like David,
the wild wind of Spirit

fanning those flames
of my large and little love?
You have set me on fire,

O my Lord, at the last,
after years of scut and cold smolder.
And I can not stop burning.

St. Saliere

"I absolve you all . . . for I am your patron saint:
the Patron Saint of Mediocrity."
                                        —*Amadeus,* Peter Shaffer

As if a bitter tongue could taste honey,
bile rising from his heart—
the ear, a vessel made for art,
were pricked with pride, waxed with envy.
As if a monk could love the world
and sing the flesh's aria,
a blind man see the sun unfurl,
the night's starry *Gloria*.
As if a saint who had no skin
could know the coals beneath his feet,
a sinner who claimed no sin
could own the joy of sin's defeat.
As if desire could serve for love,
the crow become the dove.

Black Robe's Box

October 19th, 1646
First Feast of St. Isaac Jogues

The Mohawks kept it in sacred space,
the talismanic dark where the small dead
God might be felt but never beheld.
Blind hands would kiss the mystery in secret.

Chalice, paten, crucifix,
glass cruets for water and wine,
satin stole embroidered with *fleur-de-lis,*
blue of the New World's chicory sky,

all arranged neat in the small box,
hewn from local oak, the deep-carved cross
marking the contents as holy
of holies, ark of the consecrated host.

Mon Dieu, Mon Dieu, do not forsake us.
When the corn died white in the blighted fields,
and the children shook with fever and rattled
last breaths in the arms of disconsolate wives,

one chief spoke of the Black Robe's box
left as blessing but now turned curse
killing them quietly in the dark.
He named each implement and knew its power.

Before St. Isaac returned to them,
they had martyred him daily in their minds,
employed each brutal and bloody device.
One crucifixion would never suffice.

St. Lazarus

He knit him self up, a cable-stitch of skin.
Pushed his left eye in its socket, then his right.
Cracked the knuckles in his fingers (now so thin!).
Raised him self from the dirt and stood up right.

Lazarus, Lazarus, don't get dizzy.
Lazarus, Lazarus, now get busy.
Mary's weeping, Martha's made a cake,
Jesus is calling at the graveyard gate.
Your closest cousin, happy you are dead,
Eyes Martha's sheep and Mary's empty bed.

The chorus of voices sings him awake.
Once a body's broken, it cannot break.
He licks his lips and wags his muscled tongue.
Flexes each foot till the warm blood comes.
Turns from the darkness and moves toward the sun.
A step. A shamble. A dead-out run.

Heresy #2: St. Ikaros

He always was a boy
who never listened.
When his mother,
God rest her soul,
would pull him away
from clifftop and precipice,
he would ascend again
once her back was turned.
I knew no good
would befall him.

So when the thought first flew
across my tired mind,
I batted it away
like a noisome buzz
that circles near the ear,

as if I saw beforehand
how the boy would rise and rise
on my beautiful wings,
make me proud as Pilate
the scourging didn't work,
that he would be the boy
he's always been,
smarter than most,
starved for more
than human life could give.

The last time I saw
him struck me blind,
his arms bound to the cross

bar of those wide wings,
his bare feet twined
at the ankles, delicate
as a girl's at her mirror,
a boy made exactly for this:
his whole body burnished
in a nimbus of fire,

my fine child climbing
that cliff of air and light
heading towards heaven
holding fast to his
father's false art.

III. Speaking in Tongues

The Conversation

After 10 years of correspondence, Thomas Merton and Czeslaw Milosz met briefly in a restaurant in San Francisco in October of 1968, two months before Merton's sojourn to Thailand and his sudden death. There is no record of their last conversation.

"Friendship is the most important thing, and it is the true cement of the Church built by Christ." Thomas Merton

"I am not my own friend.
Time cuts me in two." Czeslaw Milosz

"Opposition is true friendship." William Blake

I. The Saints Select a Booth by the Window Overlooking the Bay

Against the solitary gulls,
the seal lions with scepters on rocky thrones,
two enormous men in ordinary bodies
stride the hills, hungry for food that feeds
holy the imperishable heart.

To see a world in a grain of sand,
where *Christ plays in ten thousand places,*
each sets forth a foot and hand,
finds *letters from God dropt in the street.*

They stop before an open door, a sign
(I am only a man: I need visible signs)
and enter full of Dante's hope
despite the world's unwritten directive.

II. The Saints Order from the Menu, a la Carte

It is the Walt Whitman of menus.
Oil of olive, flesh of pig, raspberry-seeded sauce.
(All this I swallow, it tastes good, I like it, it becomes mine.)

The monk eyes the reluctant epicure.
I love beer and, by that very fact, the world.

He gives him that only-a-Trappist-would-say-so
look and orders vodka. Straight and cold.
*I have been devouring the world in vain
For fifty years, a thousand would not be enough.*

Breast of duck, leg of lamb, tender capon thigh.
*No one can accuse me of being without joy
Of not noticing girls who pass by.*

Radiccio, Arugula, Swiss Chard.
It's been a year since he loved the woman
As a man loves a woman.
Of this a holy poet cannot speak.

Turbulent, fleshy, sensual, eating, drinking & breeding.
It is man's nature to tire of his nature.
*Yes, I would like to be a poet of the five senses,
That's why I don't allow myself to become one.*

At home, the monks enter, *robes voluble as water.*
Each one can sit at table with his own lemon
And mind his conscience.
Of this a holy poet may speak.

He nods his head and throws back his vodka.
Yes, thought has less weight than the word lemon.
That's why in my words I do not reach for fruit.

III. Grace

So what kind of prophet am I?
Why should the spirit have visited
such a man as I've been made?
Why this Catholic need to confess myself
to every priest I find? Including you.

There is no where in you a paradise
that is no place and there
you do not enter except without a story.

My pen a knife against my heart
unrelenting against forgetting,
a hostage of my memory,
I sing myself bound and free.

Who would dare to go nameless in the universe?
Yet, to tell truth, only the nameless are at home.
They bear with them in the center of nowhere
the unborn flower of nothing.
This is the paradise tree.

He made me Milosz, you Merton,
and neither of us home
and sent us on a pilgrimage to find it.
We have seen on our way and fallen in love
With the world that will pass in a twinkling.
The maker loves the maker and the made.

IV. Meat (Fish for the Trappist)

Multiplicity my delight, your despair.
In the very essence of poetry there is something indecent:
a thing is brought forth which we didn't know we had in us,
so we blink our eyes, as if a tiger had sprung out
and stood in the light, lashing his tail.

Multiplicity your delight, my despair.
Prayer is the study of Art.
Praise is the practice of Art.
Poems the language of angels we speak.
(Sweet Christ, discover diamonds
And sapphires in my verse.
I hang thy rubies on these autumn trees,
On the bones of the homegoing thunder.)

Multiplicity my delight, your despair.
Poetry is rightly said to be dictated
By a daimonion, and the poet
A houseful of demons speaking in many tongues.
A language of angels!
Mind that you do not deceive yourself and others.
What comes from my evil—that only is true.

Multiplicity your delight, my despair.
A poem, the intuition of perfection
resembles the soul in mystical prayer.
It is still. It is one.

Multiplicity my delight, your despair.
The purpose of poetry is to remind us
how difficult it is to remain just one person.
Invisible guests leave and enter our house at will.

The best we can do is to hope that good spirits,
not evil ones, choose us for their instrument.

V. Des(s)ert

My Lord, I loved strawberry jam
And the dark sweetness of a woman's body.
And yet I cannot touch the center.
"You will never know what I feel," she said,
"Because you are filling me and are not filled."

I am only filled when I am empty.
I am the utter poverty of God.
I am his littleness, nothingness, lostness.
A self-emptying of God in me
forgets the pull of pleasure
receives the fullness of Grace.
Sometimes in quiet.
Once with electrifying force.

Sure, women have only one, Catholic, soul,
but we have two, Dionysus's and Christ's,
one forever filling, one forever full,
a poet and a man, I live between lives.

There is no now but only always.
Time is but a stream I go a-fishing in.
Casting in the shallows and reeling in stars.
Living in the nick of eternity.

VI. The Saints Depart through the Main Entrance,
   Each in His Own Good Time

A folded napkin, an empty glass
crumbs arranged in concentric rings,
the monk has left his mark on the silence.

In two months time (no, not so much as two)
he will have left the world as well. (*Terribly,
Sweet Christ, how terribly his beauty burns us now!*)

How slowly this bell tolls
in a monastery tower
for the death of a man
and of that brave illusion:
the adventurous self
from whom he sought escape in an abbey.

Slowly Milosz gathers up his belongings,
well-earned honors, several decades' worth of poems,
preparing to leave it all behind him.
This. Which signifies knocking against a stone wall
and knowing that the wall will not yield.

Soon he, too, will arise and go
through the entrance that leads to the sea
in the general direction of *Heaven*
where it must be there as it is here,
except that I will be rid of my dull senses
and my heavy heavy *bones.*

Changed into pure seeing
I will absorb as before
The proportions, the color, a Paris street,
all of it (as ever) *incomprehensible,*
incomprehensible
the multitude of (in)visible things.

St. Seamus

"I rhyme to see myself, to set the darkness echoing."
Seamus Heaney

For years I've knelt at your holy wells
and envied the cut of your clean-edged song,
lain down in the bog where dead men dwell,
grieved with ghosts who told their wrongs.

Your consonants cleave my soft palate.
I taste their music and savor it long
past the last line of the taut sonnet,
its rhyming subtle, its accent strong.

And every poem speaks a sacrament,
blood of blessing, bread of the word,
feeding me full in language ancient
as Aran's rock and St. Kevin's birds.

English will never be the same.
To make it ours is why you came.

Homage to St. Edna: A Sonnenizio

What lips my lips have kissed and where and why
are lips my lips have missed, and so I try
remembering each kiss and lovely boy,
revisiting each lip and every joy
attendant on the kiss of new desire
hung upon the smoky lip of fire.
And yet I know the where and why of love
remains unspoken by my lips and tongue,
as secret as the first kiss of the young,
as chastened as the kiss of hand in glove.
And so I seek the lips I have forgot,
each kiss bestowed by love and those by lust.
It is the why and where of both I must
relinquish with the kisses I can not.

St. Clarence

On Hearing Clarence Clemmons' Saxophone Solo
in "Jungleland," Madison Square Garden, New York

Three minutes of sweet
dark of the heart
pouring from his gold
horn of plenty,
more where that comes from,
each soul knows,
the hunger for the low note,
the throb of high heaven,
stars struck across the Spring-
steen scattered sky.

Give us our god back,
the crowd urges and surges,
beauty so old and beauty so new,
once gripped in the palm
of a gritty hand,
a smudged host,
a bolt of wine
clean as the cut
of your backstreet song.

Take us with you,
Saint of the Sax,
as you palm each rung,
climb the ladder of passion,
noche oscura,
forgetful as noon,
far as the midnight
gang's rendezvous,
the human doomed & tragic romance.

Three minutes of sweet
dark of the heart,
and ten thousand become one,
your story our own,
being and blood,
player and played,
ear & lip & aching tongue,
god-longing
heard and sung.

St. Melville

Woodlawn Cemetery, Bronx

"Wonderfullest things are ever the unmentionable; deep memories yield no epitaphs." Moby Dick

Is this what you were called to, still pilgrim,
   to sleep beneath six small feet of earth?

A scroll unrolled across your headstone
   unengraved: *the whiteness of the whale?*

Is this the *dumb blankness full of meaning*
   Ishmael fought and found at the end?

Or is it pure chance, Queequeg's oaken sword
   struck blunt across the warped *Loom of Time?*

A paradox and pleasure to find you here,
   grounded, for now, on the leeward shore,

your own bones unmarked by any writing,
   not one hieroglyph of what you'd hoped to be,

no tattoo grafted from the savage thigh,
   no etching from the dead leg of Ahab.

That you should leave us silent at the last
   like the mad captain taken by the sea

echoes and keeps your bitter promise,
   your life *but a draught,* unfinished and undone.

I place on your stone among the offerings—
    rocks and blossoms, mute things of this earth—

a shell cleft clean by the constant tide,
    the song without words she sings and sings.

St. Hawthorne

". . . your heart beat in my ribs and mine in yours, and both in God's."
Melville, letter to Hawthorne, November 17, 1851.

True-eyed, blue Nathaniel,
perturbed by love unearned,

you take Herman's hand,
his eager heat, only coldly.

What rote redundancy
brings him here, a friend

where friends are plenty-
ful and thick as thieves?

He arrives all extra-
vagance, extra-ordinary, ex-cess,

too too many stresses
in a Puritan line.

He ships you
a freighted tale of thunder,

life hulled in every wave
inked across the wide white sea.

Letters fall from the sky
like Visitations,

the child leaping
in your sudden womb.

How is it that he holds
your heart—and more,

your art—in his
open, unmatched hand?

Heresy #3: St. Ahab

Talk not to me of blasphemy, man;
I'd strike the sun if it insulted me." Moby-Dick

Old fire-lover, Jehovah-hater,
thief of men's minds, how you prosper.

These the pages of your holy book
proclaim you a devil and a god.

Baptized in savage blood,
you yearn towards murder

your weapon
a poetry of dread.

We fear and love you in your madness,
your five wounds each our own,

finding our selves full of anger,
black bile of loving what we love.

You are us, you heartless martyr,
we are you through and through,

the cock of the hammer (*squeeze and fire*),
lips pressed to the steel of the sword,

gunning the engine in red-eyed rage,
the bomb exploding in the marketplace.

How we bless our horrors with abstraction.
Vengeance. Justice. In Ahab's Holy Name.

IV. Seeing Through
   Not With The Eye

St. Emily & Botany

Emily Dickinson's Garden Exhibition,
New York City Botanical Gardens

Poems rise like Irises—
Slender girls who tell
Their secrets to the bees—

Beg our attention,
A blind man's cup
Offered you & me.

I give my eyes—
You lend your tongue—
And—word wise—gradually—

Minds collect—
And genuflect
As one who once were three.

St. Vincent

"The best way to know God is to love many things."
Vincent Van Gogh

What Vincent loved of sky he told the crows.
He taught them blue and the long note of want,
the rut and whorl of time that comes and goes,
God's face in the field, drawn and gaunt.
What Vincent loved of earth he told the trees.
Their branches writhed like flames when they heard
how every leaf and bole at last is seized
and falls like olive stones and evening birds.
What Vincent loved of salt he told the sea:
the play and savor of the friends of Christ,
their sails taut, each mast a wood-crossed T,
the empty boats afloat on waves of light.
What Vincent loved of fire he told the fire,
then placed his wounded hand upon the pyre.

Christ's Colors
Upon Passover & Holy Thursday Falling on the Same Day

Yellow, green
as risen grass,
dandelion spike,
forsythia whip,

the hue of Judas
at table, cross-
legged, urgent
to run, to kiss,

to quiet the riot
in his jaundiced heart—
shade of the silken sash
wound about Mary's head,

the lemon she used
to rinse her hair,
long as a hemp rope,
thick as a strip of hide.

Pale pink of hyacinth,
small girls'coats,
church hats,
Easter's eager daughters.

Sudden scarlet
staining the lintel
sparing the lucky
son inside.

And royal purple,
Color of Kings,
draped upon God
dark as irony.

Christ's words
amid the ink-black fact,
sweet red
blood in our mouths.

The Vigil

How did he do it?
Open those good hands,
spread his five fingers wide
to receive the blunt nails?
Hear the crack of bone,
delicate wingwork of phalanx and carpal?
Hang the weight of His whole self
from those soft clay doves
and trust them to hold?
To hold?

They flutter light.
Brush against the good wood.
His mother's eye catches,
watches as she used to watch
beside her dreaming child
those white birds of paradise
gently reach
for some thing lost,
some thing left behind,
some kingdom he saw about to come.

Mary's Promise

After John Collier's "Pieta"

I.

Heavy as a heart, this heft against my thigh.
He's grown so big I need my legs to hold
what my arms alone could once enfold,
could carry long hours beneath a wide sky
every mile of his twice-blessed life.
We clung to one another, a pair of poor
swimmers, knowing we would sink, clutching closer
as the waters rose faster, roiled higher.
Once I let him go and he walked on water,
on air, over desert—it didn't seem to matter—
he started down the road leading away
from our two-room life and grew smaller each day.
I watched him until I could not see
his body moving away from me.

II.

And I heard what my prophet's heart whispered
while my mind blinded me in her mercy—
that my son would find a wretched dying
designed for the worst of our killing kind
at the hands of men he would call *friend*
and return to his mother in the end,
the arms that held him and the legs that strode
his childhood hills to Calvary's road.
Now I have him again and I say *No*,
never again will I let him go.
Forget the tomb and its stink of earth.
I will not leave him to stone and dirt.
I'll walk him, myself, into heaven's skies.
Enclosed in these arms is paradise.

On Seeing Van Gogh's "*Sower with Setting Sun*" on the Feast Day of St. Francis

Van Gogh's sower bows his brown head.
His heavy hand scatters small seed
against a setting sun so thick
with cream and ocher, I believe
I can grasp it, place and taste it on my tongue.

Francis named Him *Brother* in the hymn
he sang daily once he lost his sight,
as if darkness made the Sun more dear,
as if song could replicate His light.

Though the wide sky grins
unearthly green, and clouds peek pink
as a conch's ear, I believe
in the coming of evening,
in the heavy hand blessing the good ground,
in the sower sainted by the sun's round.

Heresy #4: Turner's Tale

J.M.W. Turner Exhibition,
Metropolitan Museum of Art

The sun is God, he said in word and paint
over and over, his heretic hand and eye
faithful to the harsh white of Welsh light,
Madonna blue of Venice morning sky.
A God who blinds us, says the snow's swirl
overtaking Hannibal, his toy-size
elephants tamed and terrified, the whirl-
wind so fierce she mutes their war cries.
A God who watches as the Houses fall,
as red and yellow sing their bright aria,
black smoke rising from London's wall,
the towers flaming with fire's hysteria.
A God who hides as the slave ship goes down,
the bound women and their children drown.

V. Holy Ground

War Cry

There are a million ways to slaughter
innocents, our sons and daughters.

Children bursting into flames
give common death uncommon names:

Napalm,
whispers Vietnam.

Auschwitz,
hisses bone and ash.

Hiroshima,
sings the flash.

They run from war to war to war.
They cry for peace, our ancient yearning.

Again we set their world on fire.
Again they can't stop burning.

The Long Run
On my 49th Birthday

I have run along the shores of big rivers—
   Tiber, Nile, Rhine, Thames, Seine—
sucked thick Mississippi-soaked air
   into thirsty lungs, and run and run
and run, my legs thick as Caravaggio's
   saints', mounting their horses, urging the stirrups,
running from soldiers taking the Christ away.
   My heart a marvel, all those many miles,
pumping blood through winding valleys of veins,
   the creeks and streams feeding my glad flesh,
animal being ignorant of its mystery.
   Who was she, that girl with the witch-wild mane,
who ran with the world's own waters inside her
   flush and full of a love she could not name?

Big Sur Saints

New Camaldoli Monastery,
Feast of St. Benedict

Christ called so loud, we left the lonely road
that rimmed the earth along the singing sea,
a gentle summons from a gentle Friend,
sweet promise of God's hospitality.
The monks were gathered on the mountain top,
the table set, their vespers just begun,
two spaces open on the altar steps.
The echo of the single church bell rung.

Here each man chanted his best hopes aloud
like sane men singing to a world gone mad,
and our two voices joined the joyful choir
in that strange place lit by ordinary fire.
We blessed and we broke. We spoke the ancient code.
We left the holy mountain. Bread and blood for the road.

God's Gardens

"At the place where Jesus was crucified, there was a garden, and in the garden a new tomb, in which no one had been laid." John 19:41

From garden to garden, God's body moved.
Born to breath beneath Eden's tree,
He named Himself Adam, Herself Eve,
a twice-crowned exiled King and Queen.
Gethsemane came a dark surprise—
(Who knew where the garden gate might lead?)—
the wind in the olives, the moon's slow rise,
the tell-tale blood on bony knees.
That gray Friday we carried Christ home
to one last garden, while evening birds
sang a song of pity His stopped ears heard
until He rose and hove away the stone.
Our good dead God, while the dawn birds keened,
bloomed anew in the garden's sudden green.

On Pilgrimage

Glendalough Monastery, County Wicklow,
St. Kevin's Day

They're great ones for travel, the Irish Saints,
or so the map announces with its names
of mountains, towns, and holy old wells.

Brigid loved Liscannor's Hag's Head grandeur—
and the ground gushed in sympathy, healed all harm
long after she left to tend the fires of Kildare.

Patrick climbed the Croagh above Clew Bay
and hove a great bell past the edge
ringing in the era of snake-less Eire,

while Brendan rowed his Bantry boat from coast
to coast, baptizing pagans and blessing babies,
before setting out, at last, for America

like so many of his kin and kind
in centuries to come. How rare the saint
who homes, the blackbird hatching in his hand.

Dove & Olive

Today I rose East
and breathed peace,

a sweeter air,
an urgent prayer,

soft as the Mourning Dove
nesting in the olive

warms her eggs
new-made, new-laid.

The wings of the dove
oar the arc of love.

She knows
love grows.

Tree and she are one,
wing & leaf, song & sun.

Let me be the olive,
set my roots deep,

thrust my hands high
in praise of sky.

You be the dove,
wake from sleep,

set your bright eye East,
breathe peace.

Heresy #5: St. Hawk and St. Shrew

*"The forms and individual characters of living things,
of animals, of all nature . . . are canonized
by their beauty and their strength."—Thomas Merton*

He falls like bliss through the blue,
sky-eye fixed on small St. Shrew
who makes her way along the blind ground.

Creature-eater, he devours her
in his heart before a razor
talon scrapes a nape-hair of her fur.

She, shaped so exactingly for this:
the play of muscle, bone and breath
across the daily field of death.

He, of fringed and hollowed wings,
hears the wild blood that sings,
duet of the hunter and his love.

There is rapture in this holy role
St. Hawk enacts so black and fell,
good killer in a game of claim and keep.

St. Shrew's the hard and lesser part,
though dying gladly takes more art.
St. Lucifer and Christ watch and weep.

VI. Household Saints

Tell-Tale House

after Margie Crisp's Inferno at Dumbwater Creek

The fire-breathing house lights the horizon.
Her smoke ascends a fire-breathing sky.
The moon speaks her quiet light and spies on
the little lives we live until we die.
The windows tell their terror to the desert.
The clouds that drift on past don't hear at all
the aria of sorrow rising from her,
the house that rose up once and now must fall.

And the river continues in her travel,
and the grasses keep her life in their leaves,
as the house's history spools and unravels,
as her stories call to all who believe
in the power of the house to undo us,
in the power of the fire to renew us.

Waiting for Ecstasy

"Oh! no, you will see . . .
It will be like a shower of roses!"
— *St. Therese of Lisieux*

Day fades from gray to gray
while I stand here sorting colors:
hot whites, cold reds,
lukewarm blue and beige.

Prostrate before the cross,
heart pressed to the stone ground,
God speaks to her in roses
as the pail cools beside her,
the sodden sponge floating to the top.

I turn the dial and push.
Water fills the empty washer.
The force that moves my world, mute,
flows through power lines and circuits,
whose killing bolt can split a beating heart.

She lies still a long time,
knees and shoulders stiff,
crushed breasts numb,
her face a sun of love
in the blackened chapel.

Our clothes writhe and twist like the damned,
shells of our selves wrung and spun,
habits of our fanatic being.
I do little. I get nothing done.

Circling the cellar,
hands idle and empty,
I waste the hours
waiting for ecstasy.

Letters to My Heart

"My little children, your hearts are small, but prayer
stretches them."—St. Jean Mary Vianney

I.
Dear Heart,
>At last you are too full,
>a belly at the wedding feast
>whose hollowness is wholed
>before the groaning table goes quiet.

>But August sun warms my breast,
>and last night in a land-locked state,
>Walt Whitman sang in my ear,
>*The sea whispered me . . .*

>The loons make stupid jokes,
>dragonflies conjugate shamelessly,
>and a grown man smiled
>his boy's smile at me this morning.

>What am I to do,
>strict mistress, ready friend?
>There is so much prayer pressing
>these small walls,
>urgent to get in and to get out.

II.
Dear Heart,
>My body doesn't love me anymore
>and I am telling.

>She pesters me when I'm writing:
>*I'm hungry! I want a plate of Carpaccio!*

She distracts me with her whining:
Oh, our Sciatic Nerve!

she's keening even now
as I sit and write this letter.

She wakes me up at 3AM
and won't let me go back to sleep:

Let's eat chocolate cake! she says,
Let's exercise and read Thomas Wolfe!

She's full of bad ideas—
like getting fatter every year,

like singing *el-e-va-tor* in my ear
as I heave her up six flights of stairs to our office,

like swelling big as a gourd when a mosquito
steals a little drop of her precious blood—

I'm telling you, Heart, she is crazy,
and I want to be rid of her, except,

being my body and my blood,
I'd miss her more than I expect.

III.
Dear Heart,
Please be my memory
When my mind is shot.

Please show some courage
When I would rather not.

Please keep beating
Even when I sleep.

Please keep repeating,
As I swim out deep

How much you love me,
How you hold me dear.

Keep on whispering
What I want to hear.

Say *Yes*, Dear Heart,
My Liar. My Art.

IV.
Dear Heart,
       I found a hole in you today.
       Held you underwater in a shiny pail,
       watched the air bubbles, fat-bellied Buddhas,
       pop the still surface of my skin.

Dear Heart,
       I need to patch you,
       affix the criss-cross tapes to stop the breech,
       blood pumping out thick as toothpaste
       from a rhino-stomped, hippo-sat tube.

Dear Heart,
       You are a heavy fish
       a hunk of meat at the end of my line.
       Look at me, Heart.
       The Mother-of-All-Waters is talking to you.

V.
Dear Heart,

Why are you on my sleeve?
Why do I feel you rising in my throat,
pulsing in the palm of my hand
when I wish you would just lie low,
an anonymous time piece in your house of bone?

You are small, yet weigh a ton,
are hard as marble, yet light like rain,
brave in battle one day,
false and faint as any fool the next.

Dear Heart,

You are wise and winsome,
nimble as a bride.
You skip when my Beloved
lies beside me,
his face my constant sun.

You race, a wild filly
stamping at the gate,
ever ready to run
at the crack of the start gun.

Dear Heart,

You are an idiot—
You do not know your bounds.

We are a dying animal.
Our destiny is sleep.

Yet you say *No, No, No,*
with each declining beat.

Blessing

In the doorway of the empty house
the woman waits, night silent outside,
learning how to say goodbye.

The floor shines wet in the moonlight,
mop in her left hand, bucket at her feet,
right hand resting on the brass knob.

Propped up in the wood telephone box
gleams the cross of San Damiano,
the one that gave good Francis stigmata.

Alabaster Mary stands straight
in the arched niche beside it,
her infant son slung loose against her hip.

The woman's car idles in the dark
filled with her household belongings.
Her grown son sounds the horn, twice.

In Pope-like gesture, she signs
the room, echoes the words in the blue note
to the couple and their child who enter

this same doorway eight hours later.
They do not hear the blessing in the air.
They do not see the blood on the lintel.

Double Lives

Eating dinner at the new neighbors' home,
we spoke of sons and books, work we'd loved,
houses we had bought and never owned,
cars that brought us to each town and promptly died.
Later, after grappa and strawberries,
June blue lingering in the tallest trees,
the talk turned dark: cancer, friends left behind,
those ordinary lives now seeming fine.

All the while, the moon taught her slow lesson,
shading our faces with her borrowed light.
We parted four friends bound by the common
disciplines of loss and measured delight:
loving the world with only half our strength,
holding it lightly and at arm's length.

Homegoing

"I was there. I had my existence.
Me in place and the place in me."
                                    —*Seamus Heaney*

We drove those roads as if we'd always known them,
the steep ways and winding bends amazing us
at every easy turn, and all the world we'd left

behind so green, we'd forgotten how deep
the earth could be. *You'll be late for your own*
funeral, our mother used to warn us,

three daughters who disregarded time
as if its hours bound all others but ourselves.
And there we were, driving fast, her ashes

stashed in the hatch, as late for her interment
as our own, resisting the pull of the place
we'd begun, the place she was going back to be,

the small hole nicked in familiar ground,
home, three feet square and three feet down.

"And the Angel Left Her . . ."

Luke 1:38

So there she stood alone amid a stillness
as loud as any earthquake she had heard,
the eaves creaking in the absence of wind,
the hiss and tick of radiators warming
the house along with a soon-coming sun.
Her hands touch her belly, swelling already
like dough cupped close in an earthen bowl.
She knows it won't be long before she shows.
What to do with all this sudden silence?
Phone her boyfriend: *Joseph, I have news!*
Text St. Anne: *Dear Mother, I'm afraid.*
Drop to her knees, now weak with recognition
and kiss the space he filled a moment past
in answer to the question he had asked?

Afterwords

Poet's Heresy

"I feel that the Godhead is broken up like bread at the supper, and we are the pieces."—Herman Melville

I'm a Sicilan woman
and my poems say *mangia*!

I want to feed you
bread and wine, fruit and feast,

blessed and broken words
to chew, chew, chew.

I want you to eat them
purely for pleasure,

to put your lips around *p*,
crack *k*'s with your crowns,
roll *l*'s across your taste-budded tongue,

to swallow sweet & easy
the meal of your life.

For it is what your body craves,
your heart sorely wants,
what your gut loves.

It is lies & truth, death & life,
sweet/sour, adazzle/dim,

what you have always
and have never known.

It is itself and you besides,
every thing & no thing at all.

It stuffs you full and leaves you
heavy, hungry, starved for more.

It makes you glad.
It troubles your sleep.

It is my body & my blood.
Here. Take. Eat.

Notes

The Conversation

The words that appear in italics are drawn or adapted from a variety of sources. The majority of them come from the poems and prose writings of Thomas Merton and Czeslaw Milosz. In addition, the reader will recognize quotations from works by William Blake, Gerard Manley Hopkins, Henry David Thoreau, and Walt Whitman, writers admired and emulated by Merton and Milosz.

In section IV, "Meat (Fish for the Trappist)," the recurrent phrases "Multiplicity my delight, your despair" and "Multiplicity your delight, my despair" are adapted from a poem by Denise Levertov, "On a Theme by Thomas Merton."

About the Author

Angela Alaimo O'Donnell teaches English, Creative Writing, and American Catholic Studies at Fordham University in New York City where she also serves as Associate Director of the Curran Center for American Catholic Studies. She has published two chapbooks, *MINE* (2007, Finishing Line Press) and *Waiting for Ecstasy* (2009, Franciscan University Press) and a full-length collection of poems, *Moving House* (2009, Word Press). O'Donnell's poems have appeared in many journals, including *America, Bearings, Christian Century, Comstock Poetry Review, Concho River Review, Die-Cast Garden.com, First Things, Hawaii Pacific Review, New Texas, Pedestal Magazine.com, Potomac Review, RUNES: A Review of Poetry, Windhover,* and *Xavier Review.* She has been nominated for a Pushcart Prize, The Best of the Web Prize, and was a finalist for the Foley Poetry Award, the *Elixir* First Book Award, and the Mulberry Poets & Writers Award. O'Donnell lives with her husband in Bronxville, New York.

CPSIA information can be obtained at www.ICGtesting.com
Printed in the USA
270454BV00002B/52/P

9 781936 370351